A Personal Account of God's Healing

Reach
For Your
Miracle

BARBARA ANN PAYNE

Reach For Your Miracle

D1312960

by

Barbara Ann Payne

Reach For Your Miracle

Published by Select Arrow the publishing arm of United in Christ
www.unitedinchrist.co.uk

ISBN:1540535916

Cover design and interior layout: Homer Slack

Printed by CreateSpace

ACKNOWLEDGEMENTS

The following testimonies to God's healing power in my life cover the best part of the first 25 years of my walk with Jesus. Even though I have only covered a few pages. I have tried to cover each miracle as in depth as I can.

Without Jesus in my life I would not have a testimony to give so I thank HIM most of all for the wonderful things He has done and continues to do in my life.

I would like to thank Pastor Jim Sweet who taught me so much in my early Christian years and imparted a love for the Word of God that means so much to me and of course built my faith.

I thank my family who supported me through all these dark times and various members of the body of Christ who prayed me through some of these miracles. I cannot name them all.

I would like to thank Homer Slack for encouraging me to publish this book and his help in doing so by the design of the cover and the layout. I thank him and his wife for their fellowship.

I pray whoever is reading this now that you will find Jesus as Your Saviour and have experiences with Him that far surpass mine.

Table of Contents

The following testimonies to God's healing power in my life cover the best part of 25 years, even though I have only covered a few pages. I have tried to cover each one as in depth as I can.

Thank you Jesus

Foreword

My wife and I have been associated with Barbara now for over 25 years that is since she came with her husband to the Tabernacle Church in Radcliffe. I find it a pleasure to write this foreword to her testimony of the healings she has experienced during her walk with God.

The trust she has in her Saviour is truly amazing. She doesn't just believe in God, she believes God and it is that belief in what He says is the key to her remarkable testimony of not only her healings, but also her amazing exploits in her walk with God.

Read her testimony and as a result your faith in God will grow and you too will soon testify to a life of victory in Jesus.

Pastor T J Sweet (retired)
Tabernacle Church, Radcliffe.
(Now both in glory)

Chapter 1

Encounter with Jesus

———◆●◆———

I had only known Jesus a few short weeks and was very excited that God could love me, wash away my sin and give me a new life, I certainly needed it. On the outside I must have appeared very happy with two lovely boys and a handsome husband but no one knew the real me, not even my family. I had dark hidden secrets that had shaped my emotions, attitudes and way of life well into my thirties.

I will never forget the night I surrendered my life to Jesus, He instantly became real to me even though I did not understand the full implication of what I had done or why I had to do it. It was in Radcliffe Tabernacle Lancashire and Dennis (my first husband) and I had come on the invitation of his brother Mervyn. As a child I had been in the local choir in my hometown of Chesterton, Newcastle-Under-Lyme in the Church of England, but I had never heard the gospel of Jesus Christ like this before. It was such a warm, happy and vibrant church and everyone seemed so full of joy. They sang about Jesus like they knew Him and the preacher, Jim Sweet, even cried when he talked about Jesus on the cross. This was all new to me. Even though I knew nothing of the Bible I just knew everything he was saying about Jesus was true…there was an 'inner witness' that I later realised was the Holy Spirit witnessing to my spirit. I was enthralled but it was when Jim finally said 'Jesus put two arms up for you, can't you put one up for Him'? Well, my arm shot in the air as if I had been pierced through and to my delight so had my husband's. We became 'Born Again' the very same second. Well, that was our first encounter with Jesus…fantastic, and I just knew that I knew, that something special had happened to me. I also had an immediate assurance that I was heaven bound. All my past seemed to rush in front of me and I started to cry as I realised God's love had reached out to even me. I was thirty two years old. This must be the greatest, mysterious, miracle that happens to all who will believe on the Lord Jesus Christ and His atoning work upon the cross.

We began to meet regularly at the Tabernacle even though it was fifteen miles away from where we lived at the time. We just loved the music, the word and listening to what God had done in people's lives. During this time, I began having dreadful pain in my face to the point that I could not eat properly and it was even painful to smile. After attending my doctor, he pointed out that I had an arthritic jaw. Arthritis is rife in my family, so it did not come as any surprise but I thought it might have been later in life. I was quite distraught about it as my job was in sales and marketing and smiling was a great part of the job.

While in church one Sunday night Jim stopped the meeting as he 'felt' the Holy Spirit wanted to heal sick bodies. I had not witnessed this before and was in no way confident enough to go forward to the front for prayer. Anyway, a lady called Doris knew about my jaw and encouraged me to go out for prayer. I had read in the Bible that Jesus healed people and I knew He was still alive having risen from the tomb but still there was that unworthiness in me that said, I was not good enough for Jesus to do that for me, loving me would be more than enough. I did go forward and along with a few others I stood shaking with fear at what might happen. Jim anointed me with oil according to the Word of God and I returned to my seat having felt embarrassed at having to walk back down the aisle with everyone looking at me, or so I thought. I really did not expect anything from God...WOW what a surprise I had in store.

On the Wednesday, Dennis asked me if I would like to have a car ride out with him to Cheshire as he had some business to conduct. I love Cheshire and jumped at the opportunity. As with every good day out I needed some confectionery for the journey, I was very partial to a Mars Bar but had been unable to eat them since having arthritis in my jaw. I really fancied one this day so I thought to myself. " I'll just suck the chocolate and it will probably last me through to Cheshire." We stopped at the shop and by this time I was really craving for the Mars Bar.

As soon as I got it, I opened it and it tasted delicious as I gently tried to suck it. Well, after we drove a few minutes down the road I let out such a shriek that it startled my husband to the point of him slamming his brakes on. He asked what was wrong and I just stared him in the face whilst slapping my own face and blurting out **'It's gone, it's gone!'**. I had naturally started to bite and chew the Mars Bar without thinking and realised that all the pain from my jaw had disappeared................... Praise the Lord! I couldn't wait to get to Bible study to tell Jim. When I arrived at the Bible study the following Wednesday I ran up to Jim, also slapping my face, exclaiming that Jesus had healed me, there was no other explanation in my mind and I give Jesus all the glory.

As a young Christian this was a mighty act of God that caused my own faith to rise because not only did God love me but He had shown that love towards me as I dared to believe that He is alive and that He could. God met my faith. Oh by the way it never did return because in this and future healing testimonies I have come to know that **when God heals He heals, you don't have to hang on to it or be afraid of losing it or keep making positive affirmations. God said, He would, He did, and that settles it.** The testimonies, at Bible study, that Wednesday night were from all who had responded to the call for prayer on the Sunday and we had all received healing from the Lord. There was great rejoicing.

The lessons:
1. Jim heard the Holy Spirit speak to him to stop the meeting and ask those who were sick to come out for prayer.
2. He moved in faith (trusting obedience to the word of God)
3. When we heard the call from God through his servant Jim, we OBEYED in faith.
4. Follow the leading of the Holy Spirit at ALL times and see miracles happen.

Where faith lives there is no room for doubt.

Chapter 2

Baptism in the Holy Spirit

A few weeks later Jim announced there was going to be **a 'Waiting on meeting' one hour before the gospel service on the Sunday evening.** He said it was so we could receive 'The Baptism in the Holy Spirit'. I had only read about this in the Acts of the Apostles but did not fully understand what was involved or what it 'could do' to me. All I knew was, if it meant more of Jesus then I wanted it.

We went along to this meeting where people were speaking in a funny language, I later learned this is 'The Gift of Tongues' and there was no way I would be able to do that. As we started to praise the Lord and get lost in His presence, Jim started to encourage us to open our mouths as

God would fill us if we believed. Well, Dennis was first to be filled and I must confess I felt jealous because I did not think it would happen to me. As I began to get lost in Jesus, focus on what He had done for me and realise He was alive and was willing to baptise me, if I was willing to receive it, I suddenly lost my fear and it was replaced by faith. One tongue came from within me and at first I thought this was me not God, I dared to believe it was God and suddenly I knew this was Holy Spirit. **We went away on cloud nine that night after all everything would be wonderful now wouldn't it?**

We now had a deeper yearning for prayer and as I knelt before the Lord I would begin to speak in tongues. I got hold of a book, called '**I Dared to Call Him Father**' and the witness of this Islamic woman made me want to know Jesus in this way. **I needed to know how to pray like this woman.** I asked the Lord to teach me how to pray and through a book by Evelyn Christenson called '**What happens when Women Pray**' I started to follow the teaching, it was incredible how the Lord used that book to teach me. That book changed my prayer life it was an exciting time for both of us. Everyone we seemed to pray for became 'born again'. There was nothing our God could not do. We witnessed daily for Jesus and saw many people come to Him, not as many as we would have hoped for though. Our children also would join us in prayer daily they too speaking in tongues and witnessing at a very young age. We would be in prayer for as long as up to two hours together and I would spend every day at least two to three hours praying for God to change me and make me more Christ like. What I had not bargained for was the enemy of Jesus, satan himself. We did not understand that we were in a war and the Lord was preparing us for this.

****

As we attended the Bible study we got more and more hungry for God's word we bought our own Bibles and would sit up for hours reading and sharing with each other revelation after revelation of God and His word in the form of Jesus. In Romans it states *'Faith comes by hearing and hearing by the word of God.'* Little did we realise that our faith was being built up as we enjoyed God's word, the joy and challenges it brings to change our lives. We just wanted to live for Him and serve Him with all our hearts. Jim was a tremendous anointed teacher of God's word and he could really feed you. He was a real Pastor.

We decided to move house and this led us away from Radcliffe to a place called Westhoughton near Bolton in Lancashire and we started to attend a small fellowship there. It was easier for the children also to attend Sunday school as the church was more local for them. The house we moved to was very old and it was while we lived there that we experienced many strange encounters with the enemy and also angelic beings. It was here that Dennis encountered an angel. It was here we saw many souls come to Jesus, our home was God's home night and day, no wonder we came under attack from the enemy. It was here we prayed for hours on end crying for the lost souls of our family, we saw over twenty of Dennis's family come to Christ within two years.

It was while living here we contacted Jim Sweet again and asked if he would give us Bible studies on the book of Revelation, our own little church had no Pastor at the time. We thought it would only take six weeks or so as we needed this information to help us as we were having Jehovah's Witnesses coming to see us and I thought they knew more of the scriptures than Dennis and I. We soon discovered that they did not know Jesus. Of course Jim agreed and we attended his and Joyce's home most Wednesday's for almost three years. As I recall we were on Revelation,chapter 13 after three years. You see we learned that when you study Revelation you study the whole of scripture. Those were wonderful exciting days learning more about Jesus. Jim and Joyce carried on teaching from their home until they were called home to be with the Lord,. They were faithful, servants of the Lord.

As for Dennis and myself we did not understand that a couple serving the Lord, Baptised in the Holy Spirit are a danger to satan and his hosts and that we needed to be prepared for the days ahead. Satan was out to try to destroy us and **had we not been rooted and grounded in God's word** I think he might have succeeded. I now understand the words of Jesus *'Man cannot live by bread alone but by every word that proceeds out of the mouth of God'.*

At this point I can share many miracles of faith that God performed in and through our lives, perhaps another time as this is dedicated to the healing power of God in my life.

The Lessons:

1. Read, read, read, God's word (from the Bible) it is a lamp unto our feet
2. Obey God's word. Obedience is better than sacrifice and it leads to freedom
3. Pray without ceasing for souls
4. Learn from others with an anointed gifting from God
5. Put on the full armour of God praying always in the Spirit
6. Whatever you ask in Jesus's name, pertaining to the kingdom will be given unto you

Chapter 3

No Cure

We were enjoying tremendous times in The Holy Spirit, people were coming to our home and getting saved, healed and baptised in The Holy Spirit and this was **normal for us.** As far as we were concerned when anyone heard about Jesus they would automatically 'get saved' we did not expect anything less.

Of course, there were many trials and difficulties but we always found the solution in the Bible. We didn't always want to do it but we found whenever we obeyed in these difficult circumstances God brought us through and we were freed from what had tried to get a foothold, praise His name!

During this exciting time, not long after being baptised in The Holy Spirit and before we moved to Westhoughton, I began experiencing some terrible nightmares and then one night I awoke and could not move. I tried to speak but nothing came out of my mouth. As I tried to awaken Dennis I became afraid as I knew no sound was coming out

9

of my mouth. I eventually made a noise and this awakened Dennis, when he looked at me I could see from his face something was wrong. It felt as though my face was twisted and saliva was coming out of my mouth. All I could think of during this time was Jesus, I knew He was there and it was as if my body was rising to the ceiling towards a bright light. My brain was acutely aware of what was going on and I could hear and understand what Dennis was saying to me but I was unable to respond. **Terror struck me.**

With help from Dennis, I came round wondering what on earth had happened. When I eventually came round I began to cry with relief. I felt exhausted and helpless and Dennis was rubbing my arms and legs to help me move. For a couple of days later I was drained and worried because although this was new to me I was left with a 'familiar feeling' that I could not put my finger on. This was the beginning of an horrific illness and it started to destroy me mentally, physically and emotionally.

Jesus had graciously healed me of an arthritic jaw as a new Christian so I knew and had tasted of the goodness of God. All I had to do now was pray and He would heal me; wouldn't He?

These attacks/seizures started to become more frequent so whenever there was an altar call in church I would be the first at the front. Daily, in my own prayer life, I would ask the Lord to heal me but heaven seemed like brass. I was reading God's word at every opportunity as I became hungry to know the Jesus who had passionately saved my soul through the shedding of His Precious, Divine blood. We were seeing souls saved in our families and I was even laying hands on the sick, in faith, and Jesus healed them (James 5. 13-16)

These seizures were now happening two to three times a week and I was afraid to go to sleep at night as this is when it happened. I was also afraid to tell anyone. I heard well meaning Christians – from the pulpit –preaching that you must be in sin if you are suffering in sickness. I couldn't believe it! This wasn't the God I had read about. I examined my life and of course fell short, the Bible says *"We have all sinned and fall short of the glory of God."* (Romans 3.23).

Eventually we went to a doctor, privately, and after many tests I was diagnosed, Nocturnal Epilepsy and Sleeping Paralysis of which, he said, was **no cure.** I was devastated and desperate. He prescribed some medication and for the first time in a long time I slept peacefully. This peacefulness was not without payment because after three short weeks I knew I had become addicted to the drugs and moreover the seizures returned. At £40 a time I could not afford to return to the doctor. I was now in a worse state than before having seizures and addicted to drugs that were having no positive results. I was still hungrily reading God's word and praying, believing God would heal me and yet feeling I must not be a good enough Christian – not doing enough – not worthy enough for God to heal me of this. I became of a mind to take my own life because at thirty five I did not want to live the rest of my life in that state.

I have always loved Jesus since becoming 'born again'. He introduced me to a life of faith, fun and a future in Him and the longer I served Him the sweeter He grew. I used to say to Dennis only if this is for the glory of God can I endure. This went on for five years.

One Saturday night I had a terrible seizure and on the Sunday morning I was exhausted and wanted to stay in bed. Dennis would normally leave me to sleep it off but this morning was different he encouraged me to try to get up so we could go to church. He said it was the best place for me to be. We arrived late and sat at the back and towards the end of the meeting I sensed The Holy Spirit say to me **"Ask the elders to lay hands on you"** In the other ear came a response "You've done that a few times but it hasn't worked has it?" Well I knew which one is in the word of God and it wasn't that one. The Bible says, "obedience is better than sacrifice", so after the meeting I asked Willie Hacking, a dear friend of Smith Wigglesworth, and a Godly saint to pray for me.

People were busy coming and going and Mr Hacking had no idea what was wrong with me, he didn't need to, God knew. He prayed a simple prayer of faith and I went home. There were no flashing lights or clashes of thunder **Just faith.** After all, I had asked for prayer so many times why should this be any different? As the day moved on and bedtime approached I reached for my tablets when I heard a still small voice (not audible) in my spirit, say these words "trust me Barbara". That's the first time I remember God calling me by name and at that moment looking back I had a choice yet again to listen to God or carry on taking my medication. I decided to trust the Lord, after all if I died through one of these seizures I would win and if I lived I would win, because I would be with God either way.

From that day to this, I stand as a testimony to the greatness of God and His healing power in the 21st century. **I have never suffered since** almost forty years later.

Once when I was sharing this testimony with someone I said it took five years for God to heal me and the Lord checked me in my spirit saying to me,...."1000 years is but a day to the Lord, I heard you the same day you cried out".

GOD ANSWERS PRAYER. Amen

The lessons:

1. Pray without ceasing, never doubting
2. Listen to God's word alone
3. Never give up
4. Give God the glory always be willing to testify of His greatness
5. Perfect love casts out fear

Caution:

I only stopped taking medication because God had spoken to me personally. I do not advocate anyone stopping their medication without their doctor's advice.

Chapter 4

Delivered from Smoking

---◆•◆---

When I first got saved at Radcliffe I was smoking forty cigarettes a day. I would have at least five in the morning along with a pot of tea. I remember visiting the doctor and he told me that, after examining my chest, he would not like to examine me ten years on. I was in my early thirties then. I really didn't take much notice of that after all nothing happens to you does it, it happens to other people. Well, after my 'born again' experience the urge to smoke left me. I only wish I could say that I didn't start again, but I did.

The more I studied God's word the more convicted I became to give up smoking but I did not find this easy at all. I was getting to the point of paranoia as I knew the Lord wanted me to stop abusing my body. Oh! I used to be very opinionated about drug addicts and how they had no will power and how disgusting they were until one day when I was so desperate to stop this smoking, I sensed the Lord tell me, 'but you are a drug addict'. I was shocked but **He was right.** Coming to terms with this was awful because I could not give them up. Knowing God hears and answers prayer I began asking Him to help me as I wanted to be a good witness for Him. Every time I picked up my Bible I would read 'Holiness as unto the Lord' this did not mean because I smoked I was not holy although at the time I thought it did. No! God wanted obedience from me in this matter and I could not do it. I felt so ashamed I was saying I will do anything you ask of me Lord and there I was unable to give up smoking for Him.

Over a six month period I became more and more desperate until one night in our church an appeal was given for people to come out to the front for prayer. I was ashamed to tell anyone that I wanted to give up smoking as I thought they would have seen me as a failure in Jesus and I did not want to let Jesus down. How funny, when they must have smelled the nicotine on me. Anyway this night in fear and trembling I went forward for prayer. I managed to tell the pastor that I needed to stop smoking and do you know what? He didn't even pass a comment or seemed perturbed in any way. As he began to pray for me I felt so sick and desperate before my God that eventually this awful scream came from within me, I was horrified that people had heard me as I was a quiet person back then. I had no idea what had happened to me, I don't think anyone else did either. I know now though. I never suffered any withdrawal symptoms from forty a day to this day. God delivered me from this addictive hold on my life that I believe was a demon. I do not want to enter into any theological debates on this or any other part of my testimony, because it is a testimony that when God is present by His Spirit with desperate souls, **He hears their cries,** and delivers them from the evil one. Thank you Jesus.

The lesson :
1. To be honest about our addictions
2. To believe when God has spoken
3. Most of all TO TRUST IN HIS DELIVERANCE
4. God never lets us down

Thank you Jesus.

Chapter 5

Angina

We moved from Westhoughton to Grimsby which is also a tremendous testimony to the Lord.

We had been serving at the church in Grimsby for a couple of years, involved in the praise and worship team, praying groups, evangelistic outreaches besides running a home group. Dennis worked full time too and I worked in the church office a few hours a week besides the card shop. I was really enjoying this kind of life; I thought this was the 'Acts of Apostles' church that I had so longed for.

I remember not feeling too well the morning I went to the office to type up missionary letters for the pastor as he was going into hospital that week. It was my son Wayne's birthday the day after and I had decided to go to town after the office to buy Wayne a birthday present. One of the sisters came into the office and 'tore a strip off me' for something I had not done and I had tried to talk to her but she did a 'hit and run' routine. Knowing that we must keep short accounts with one another I tried to go after her but she continued to shout and rode off on her bike. This left me feeling worse and I thought that I would ring her when I got back from the shops and explain that her assumptions were unfounded.

Well, I managed to walk to town and bought some trousers for Wayne's birthday and went to a café and ordered baked potato with chilli. I felt exhausted and never thought about ordering a taxi home, I just decided to walk back. When I arrived home I slumped in the chair as I was having chest pains. I managed to telephone my friend Karen who lived a couple of streets away and she came right away. She rang for an ambulance and the next thing I knew I was in hospital. All kinds of things were going through my mind as the nurse placed an oxygen mask over my face, and after many tests I was taken to coronary care. After a week I was transferred to one of the main wards but I still felt weak and very vulnerable and waiting for a diagnoses of what had happened to me. Dr. Jones who was my consultant was wonderful when he did the rounds, he came to me with his 'entourage' and explained to me what was wrong. He told me I had Angina and that they were sending me to Hull hospital to detect exactly where they were going to operate. He told me there was a possibility of two different types of procedures. As he was explaining all this, it was like his voice became an echo and I was in a different time zone looking on to everything and just nodding in the right places. I was in shock; I was too young to have heart trouble, I had too much to do, I had meetings organised and we were planning outreach events that I was terribly excited about. **I can't have this, not now.**

I was kept in hospital another two weeks and during this time I kept praying and trying to come to terms with what I had to decide. I spoke to several nurses, and asked about the by-pass operation, how it affected people and did it work? Eventually, I decided no knife was going in me and that the only knife would be the 'Sword of the Spirit', which is the Word of God.

I believed that Jesus could heal me, of course I did but no matter how I tried I did not receive any rhema word from the Lord. I had medication in the form of a spray under my tongue when the pain increased and also tablets. I also took advice from my dad to claim sickness benefit, which I did not want to do. Anyway, I found the number and began communication with the government office responsible for paying out in these situations. They were very understanding as I did not know the system and what to do. I prayed and asked the Lord for help. Not long after I received a back payment cheque of over £700.00 and a payment book to draw money every week. Although this was wonderful I preferred to have my health. I continually prayed and tried to have as normal a life as possible until my appointment came from Hull Hospital.

As summer approached, my friend Elaine asked me if I would like to go to the Assemblies of God conference, in Wales, with her and the family. I accepted but I found the week a bit difficult because I could not enter into some of the activities.

One night in the main assembly rooms, I cannot even remember who was speaking but I remember God speaking to me. The speaker mentioned that sometimes we do not receive a word from God for our situation but we just have to keep trusting and walking in faith. He mentioned Abraham and all of a sudden the Lord said to me **'This is your Isaac walk'. I remembered that Isaac believed his father right up to the minute he was placed on the altar. Then God provided a way out. I knew I had to trust God right up to the operating table and**

God would provide a way out.

Eventually my appointment came through for the beginning of the following year, the system is very slow. I thought the appointment was January but on looking again it was the February. In between these months we attended a Full Gospel Businessmen's Dinner in Hull. The speaker was Alan Jones, the man who had brought Dennis to the reality of Jesus just after we were saved. So we were looking forward to going. Alan spoke on healings for most of the night especially healing of heart disease. Naturally, I went forward for prayer and do you know, I knew something had happened but no way I could prove anything...I just kept walking in faith... a couple of weeks later I went into Hull hospital for tests overnight. That in itself was a wonderful way that God showed me that His presence was with me. I was quite scared of having this angiogram as the hospital had described in the letter to me what they were going to do and it sounded very painful. It wasn't though.

As I got on the examination table I was told to lie with my hands behind my neck and to keep perfectly still. This was it... **I was on the table. 'Now what God'?**

There were monitors around the room that I could see too as I was awake for this procedure. A very nice doctor reassured me and a kind nurse held my arm. I could see the doctor looking at the screens and then looking at my doctor's notes, then looking at the screen and then the notes. This continued for a while until finally he spoke to me and said these fantastic words. **'We cannot find anything at all'** YES! Hallelujah! Hallelujah! I kept saying this with tears of relief in my eyes.

I contacted the government department that was paying me sick benefit and told them I did not need any more financial help as God had healed me. I will leave it up to your imagination as to the response I received. I was invited to go for a medical check up and sure enough I was now free from pain.

Thank you Jesus for yet another miracle.

The Lesson:
1. Believe God right up to the end

Chapter 6

Gall Bladder

---◆•◆---

When we lived in Bolton I experienced some severe pains underneath my right shoulder blade. These just started as an ache but then developed as I was obviously accommodating the pain. I then began experiencing nausea and a loss of appetite and so I thought it best to visit the GP. I was diagnosed as having Gall Bladder problems and put on a fat free diet. Apparently, the Gallbladder's job is to deal with and separate fat from the food in the digestive tract so the doctor said this would give the gallbladder a rest. A great way to diet. I was given an appointment at the hospital in the New Year

Well, I loved butter at that time and really missed hot buttered toast, but of course I was not allowed to eat any fat. One night as I was reading my Bible I was at the end of Mark's gospel reading the great commission. All of a sudden this word became ALIVE.

<u>'you shall eat any deadly thing and it will not harm you'</u>

When God's word had spoken to me in the past like that I knew the only thing to do was to obey.....so I did. I asked Dennis to make me some hot buttered toast. He could not believe it. I explained that the Lord had spoken to me, it was very real. Fat was quite deadly to me as it gave me a lot of pain. Needless to say the rest is history. My Gallbladder showed up okay. Once again the word of the Lord had gone forth and healed me. Thank you Lord.

The lesson:
1.   God's word is trustworthy, when mixed with faith miracles happen

Chapter 7

Hidden Secrets

———◆●◆———

As I mentioned at the beginning I had dark hidden secrets that had shaped my life, but I thought I had dealt with them and that everything must disappear when you come to Jesus. What was about to happen to me was beyond my comprehension but now I know that God's word truly is a light that shines in dark places and when we let Him shine this light in our hearts He will deliver us from evil. (This was during the time that I had also had epilepsy).

This part of my testimony is not easy for me to put down on paper as some of my own family are not aware of what I am about to unfold.

Before I met Dennis and had become a Christian I had been married before. The relationship had gone wrong and during that marriage there were rows and arguments that I could not understand. My husband had become quite aggressive and he did not want to try to do anything to put it right. We were simply too young and theses difficult situations needed mature responses.

I do not believe everything is either God or the devil we have responsibility for our own behaviour.

Even though Dennis and I had become Christians a similar pattern, as in my previous marriage, had started to develop in our relationship. I could not understand this, especially since we now had Jesus in our lives and I was very happy with him and my two sons. However, being ill with epilepsy did not help either.

One day we had a telephone call from one of my best friends, Carol, she had not been saved long and Dennis and I had brought her and her husband to Jesus so we had quite a special relationship. Carol wanted to see me privately.

As we sat in our back room having tea and biscuits she suddenly started to cry. She explained how difficult this was going to be for me and for her but that God had told her to say these words to me **'there is something in your past that is preventing you from moving on and causing problems in your marriage.'**

WELL!! I could not believe this and I blurted out that it was not true and how could that be when it's Den's fault in the marriage and there is nothing from my past. You see I was covering up and soon I broke down, Carol was lovely, she offered to help me and we began to talk. She thought it would be a good idea for me to see a counsellor and that she would go with me. As a friend I knew she loved both Dennis and I and that it had taken her three months to be obedient to God as she valued our friendship and was nervous in case it was not right. Carol…thank you.

We arranged to see the doctor and he referred me to the counsellor, I was very nervous. When I entered the counsellor's office I nailed my colours to the mast. I told her I was a Christian with faith in Jesus and that I did not need to be there as I knew exactly what was wrong with me.

'Oh' she said, 'what's that then'?

'I was continually raped by my uncle when I was a little girl', I said.

Oh no I had told someone now I was bound to be in trouble. I had never told anyone I wasn't supposed to, it had been my secret for 36 years.....................I thought I had dealt with it. When I started to sob and sob and sob, I was inconsolable.

I left that office in a terrible state but somehow felt a little better for talking but also guilty as being a Christian I should let Jesus deal with it.. little did I know then that He was doing just that.

I saw the counsellor once more and then felt it right to stop. She had helped me face some very difficult issues but I did not want to carry on. I still kept asking God one last question in this nightmare. **Why was I so terribly afraid to be on my own?....** This was part of the problem in my marriage. Den could not go anywhere for long as I would have to find out where he was and when he would be coming home. I just needed him there all the time. He was suffocating.

One night, I was awakened bolt upright and God gave me the answer to my question. **You are afraid to be alone because when you were left alone it was then your uncle would abuse you.** One of God's names is Wonderful Counsellor. That night He proved that to me and the fear left me.

However, I thought it was all over. I was dealing with issues and learning to face difficulties in a more positive way.

As a young Christian I was invited to a Women's Aglow meeting in Chorley, Lancashire. I thought it was the most fantastic outreach and wanted to start one in Westhoughton. I invited a lady to come and stay with me and also to pray with me for the town. I soon realised that this lady Sheila was with me for a more important reason. As I unfolded my testimony to her she explained that she would not usually visit someone on their own but that the Lord had spoken to her to come to me but she did not know why until I got to the part of my testimony that I had been abused. She said we would talk more the following day. I was really looking forward to it as I was still a young Christian and loved listening to mature Christians.

When I arose the following morning , Tuesday 21st February 1989 and saw my boys off to school I started to feel very uneasy. I did not want to pray and did everything I could not to sit down with Sheila and talk. Well, eventually we did pray and she gently told me she was going to pray 'differently' and not to be afraid just keep looking to Jesus. I was afraid but somehow I knew what she was doing was right. She spoke to the spirit within me saying, 'come out of her'. With that the most unholy scream came out of me as I yielded my spirit to Jesus just trusting Him. That day I was delivered from a spirit of terror, an old spirit within me caused from the abuse in my young years. I fell back into the chair and became very sleepy and peaceful. Now I was free hallelujah!

What I am telling you happened over a period of time and just when I thought I was healed from this, the Holy Spirit started to teach me about forgiveness.. real forgiveness.. You see I did not want my uncle to go to heaven I wanted him to rot in hell but as I read Luke's gospel on: **Love your enemies, bless them that curse you, pray for them that despitefully use you** I knew I had not forgiven my uncle, more than that I felt justified at not forgiving him, everyone could understand that, all except God. **You see you can't just obey a bit of God's word it's all or nothing and sometimes we are asked to obey difficult commands, when we do not want to.**

I kept trying to avoid this part of God's word because I knew it had spoken into my heart, I knew I had to do it. I prayed and asked Jesus to help me to forgive my uncle but I could not feel as if I had forgiven him. Then we heard that he had cancer. Guess who got the burden to pray for him?...Yes, you are right, me. When I started to pray I knew I was not sincere, but I kept on praying in obedience. Then I decided I would have to visit him and tell him he needed Jesus and tell him what he did to me and how it had affected my life and my family. He lived over one hundred miles away from us but armed with my Bible I went.

When I arrived at his home I saw this feeble old man lying frightened of dying and I sensed Jesus' compassion for him. At that moment, all the anger left me, I knew I was free. At last the memory could hurt me no more.

I learned that forgiveness is painful and an ongoing process and it is not easy. Jesus knows that more than anyone He hung on the cross of Calvary shedding His own blood for the whole world. He uttered the words, 'Father forgive them for they know not what they do'. He meant those words.

Jesus forgave me and died for my sin, loving me when I was not even aware of Him. How can I not forgive? I learned that no matter how we feel that if we just try to be obedient to God's word then, The Holy

Spirit comes alongside us to help us fulfil the Word and bring it to pass. There was only one thing left to do and that was to tell my own father what had happened to me as a child. This was more difficult than you can imagine. Even in middle age you still care about what your parents think of you and you still want to be and feel accepted. I felt that if I told my dad he would not love me anymore. (The story is quite a long one). My mother suffered Parkinson's disease and was on holiday with a special care unit, this also gave my dad some respite as he was her full time carer. As far as I was concerned he had enough to worry about without what I had to tell him.

I decided to stay with my dad for a week while my mother was away. I was going to tell him everyday but never quite got around to it. Before I knew it my mother was going to arrive home and I still had not told my dad. It was only hours before she was due to arrive home and I could not tell my mother as it was her brother who had abused me and I could not do anything to hurt her. She was having a bad time with her health after all, I had kept this to myself all these years. Why should I upset my mother now?

While I was making a cup of tea for my dad and myself he kept going on and on about visiting my uncle when my mum got home, how she would enjoy seeing him, he never seemed to shut up and the words were resounding in my ears. The Lord really had to give me a final push. Suddenly the words were out, 'I don't think that is such a good idea dad' I said.

All of a sudden my dad stopped, looked at me and said very softly 'Why? I wasn't expecting this I didn't even expect him to hear me but it was if he was waiting for me to tell him something. I said it would be better if we just went and sat down and that it was extremely difficult to say to him what I had to say. By this time I was choking with tears and unable to get a lot of words out of my mouth. My dad sat patiently as I asked him not to interrupt me as it had taken me 36 years to tell him this. When I had completed what I had to say he just said 'why did you never say anything before? He loved me through it. **Now I felt completely free.**

Approximately eight years later I had been the President of Women Aglow Grimsby for about three years and I was invited to speak at Women's Aglow in Chorley. This was great for me as this chapter of Aglow had meant so much many years before and I considered it a privilege to share my testimony. I thought it would be a good idea to travel to Stoke-on-Trent to see my dad first and then travel up to Chorley taking a few days out to see some friends. I had been reading John's gospel chapter twenty and no matter how I tried I kept looking at verses 19-23. I prepared notes on this assuming this was for the meeting at Chorley.

I felt a need to visit my uncle during this time as I thought he needed a chance to repent. Time had done a great healing in me, so I telephoned my dad on the Thursday to tell him I would visit him on the Saturday to which he was delighted. My dad had never mentioned my uncle's name to me from the day I had told him about the situation all those years ago, but this day he told me my uncle was dying. I now started to believe that God was in this somewhere.

When I arrived at my dad's I took him for tea and we then went to the hospital, up to this point we did not know what was wrong with my uncle. He had been moved to a side ward and his family were obviously at his bedside. I felt awkward because everyone was unaware of what was going on and I was unsure of what I had to do or say. How could I ask him to repent as he was semi conscious and unable to speak as he had suffered a stroke. He also had Parkinson's disease that eventually took my mother.

During the visit my dad mentioned that he remembered getting my uncle a job and at this my uncle stirred like he had heard and was trying to respond. This now told me he could hear what was going on. I still did not know what I had to do but as I started asking the Lord for direction, He gave it to me.

We were leaving when suddenly I asked my aunt if I could have a minute on my own with my uncle and she obliged by asking everyone to leave the room. As the door closed behind them here I was, alone at last with my abuser. In the quiet of the room I felt nothing, no anger, no love, absolutely emotionless which surprised me. I said "Now what Lord?" I motioned forward to the bedside, leaned over to this dying man and whispered in his ear, These are the words that came from my mouth. " Uncle…It's Barbara here and I know you can hear me. I have come to tell you that I remember the things you did to me as a little girl and that I have forgiven you. But a greater one than I forgives you and His name is Jesus. May God grant you His peace, God bless you", and I left the room. I felt nothing not even relief because I had forgiven him years ago. So, why did I have to come now?

On the Tuesday night I gave this testimony at the Aglow meeting along with the scriptures from John's gospel. It was a great night and some women were definitely ministered to by the Lord. It was at this time I learned that my uncle had died. How great is our God, grace and more grace.

During the night I was awakened by the Holy Spirit and the word of God became so alive it was amazing. I now understood the words of Jesus when He said in John Chapter 20 verse 21 -23:

"As the Father has sent me so I am sending you". *And with that He breathed on them and said "Receive the Holy Spirit and IF you forgive anyone his sins they ARE forgiven: IF you do not forgive them, they are not forgiven"*

The lessons:

1. Wow! What I had just learned was priceless. You see it mattered that I had forgiven him but it was more important that the one who is forgiven knows he is forgiven.
2. It's the message of the cross God has forgiven us our sin by sending Jesus to pay the price. But we have to know that we are forgiven. Accept him today.
3. Invite Jesus into your heart He has forgiven you. *"God so loved the world that he gave his only begotten son that whosoever believes in him shall not perish but have everlasting life."* (John 3 v 16)

****

I know from personal experience that to forgive brings freedom. Jesus bought our freedom with His own life, BUT He is not dead, no He arose from the grave the other side of eternity that you and I could also inherit eternal life. When we accept Jesus into our heart and feed ourselves on His Word He writes our name in the **Lambs Book of Life.** He also states in Revelation that if your name is not in the Book of Life you will be cast into a lake of fire. (Revelation chapter 20)

As you read this testimony to God's grace in my life know that Jesus died for your sins too. Make sure your name is in the Lambs book of Life open your heart to Him and ask Him to come into your life today. Whatever our circumstances or situation the Lord is always near to help and lift us out of the miry clay. I do not think I would be alive today but for Jesus. I know I would not be going to Heaven either.

But now old things have passed away, behold all things are new, and the Holy Spirit is ever with us for always. Amen

Chapter 8

Reach for Your Miracle

———◆●◆———

"Go home to your friends and tell them what great things the Lord has done for you and how He has had compassion on you." **Mark 5: 19**

I have trusted and believed in Jesus Christ for over 40 years now and He has never let me down not once and it is with a very grateful and thankful heart that I wanted to record some of the miraculous things He has done, not only in my body but in my family, finances and most of all in me. So far it has been an incredible journey, one which will only end when I see my Jesus face to face. My desire then is for Him to say to me 'well done thou good and faithful servant'. I want you to know from the outset that I am nobody special but I have a special God who is as real to me today as He was when I had my first encounter with Him, if not more so. (Encounter with Jesus Chapter 1)

In Luke chapter eight we have an account of another woman in desperate need and when we read these accounts we should stop and think of the situations, culture and times that we are reading about so we get a better understanding of what is actually going on. This story actually happened. This account is well over 2000 years ago it was in the Middle East and there was definitely no National Health Service.

Here we have a woman who by faith dares to go out and try to reach Jesus. To even touch Him. She had suffered with bleeding for **12 years** and spent all her money to no avail.

No one on earth could cure her.

****

The woman's condition, which is not clear in terms of a modern medical diagnosis, is translated as an "issue of blood" in the King James Version and a "flux of blood" in the Wycliffe Bible and some other versions. In scholarly language she is often referred to by the original New Testament Greek term as the **haemorrhoissa** *(ἡ αἱμορροοῦσα, "bleeding woman").*

Because of the continual bleeding, the woman would have been constantly regarded in Jewish law as a niddah or menstruating woman, and so 'ceremonially unclean'. In order to be regarded as clean, the flow of blood would need to stop for at least 7 days. Because of the constant bleeding, this woman lived in a continual state of uncleanness which would have brought upon her social and religious isolation. (taken from Wikipedia under issue of blood)

- She could not have children
- She could not marry
- She was not supposed to be near anyone never mind Jesus
- In the old Leviticus laws of Moses she was considered unclean and everyone who came near her would have been labelled unclean and had to wash after being with her.
- So I guess she did not have many friends either.
- Here we see a very lonely, penniless, hurting desperate woman.
- She experienced shame at every turn.

We can see how she tried to hide from Jesus too how she tried to sneak up behind Him in a very large crowd hoping He would not see her. But her heart cry was, **"If only, if only, if only"**. I don't think we see anywhere else in the wonderful miracles that Jesus did, anyone else display such a cry of desperation and yet no words would pass from her lips they were coming from her heart. Not everyone in the crowd would have been a follower of Jesus some would have been curious, taking a look to see who He was and what He could do. Just like today there would have been sceptics waiting to see what He would do if anything. The religious leaders would have been there too hoping He would fail as their reputation was very important to them. But this woman had something very special. **Faith** to believe Jesus was who He said He was and belief that He could heal her. This is not a head belief this is a heart belief.

Even though she tried to hide from Him she couldn't...why? **Because He felt virtue flow from Him, He felt her faith, He knew someone had touched Him.** What fear gripped her when He said those immortal words, **'who touched me'**?

****

*"But as He went, the multitudes thronged Him. Now a woman, having a flow of blood for twelve years, who had spent all her livelihood on physicians and could not be healed by any, came from behind and touched the border of His garment. And immediately her flow of blood stopped. And Jesus said, 'Who touched Me?' When all denied it, Peter and those with Him said, 'Master, the multitudes throng and press You, and You say, 'Who touched Me?' But Jesus said, 'Somebody touched Me, for I perceived power going out from Me.' Now when the woman saw that she was not hidden, **she came trembling; and falling down before Him, she declared to Him in the presence of all the people the reason she had touched Him and how she was healed immediately.** He said to her, 'Daughter, be of good cheer; your faith has made you well. Go in peace.'"* (Luke 8 verse 42 – 48)

****

You will notice in this story that the disciples and the crowd were not aware of this faith or virtue only the woman and Jesus.

The lesson:
1. God is the same Yesterday Today and Tomorrow - **He changeth not**
2. Even in the midst of a crowd **you** can reach Jesus and **He can reach YOU**

About the Author

Barbara has been passionate for Jesus since her encounter with Him over 40 years ago and was immediately drawn into the Holy Bible where she found that the truth really does set you free from anxieties and sickness. She has taken God at His word in His healing power where she has been healed of many illnesses including epilepsy.

For over 30 years she has set up and led intercessory prayer groups, women's ministry, led in worship, ministered the gospel in song. She also preaches the gospel as well as teaching Discipleship whilst also co-pastured a church in Rochdale. At present she lives in Grimsby with her husband John she has two sons and 4 grandchildren. Barbara is still leading people to Christ and preaching the gospel as He alone is the only answer to Life.

In a synopsis, she is an intercessor, worship leader, bible teacher and minister.

Contact Me

I would love to hear your testimony after reading this book:-

Email me
paynebarbara7@gmail.com

Printed in Great Britain
by Amazon